Thinking Christians and our LGBT Neighbors

James R Black

ISBN: 979-8-90252-222-5   (Paperback)
ISBN: 979-8-90252-223-2   (Hardcover)
ISBN: 979-8-90252-221-8   (eBook)

Printed in the United States of America

DEDICATION

My gratitude goes out to the many people who helped bring this book into being and encouraged me to share it. Among them are Ashley and Jack Hernandez; several gay organists who served faithfully in my churches and kept both the music and my spirits lively; those who, as adults, completed the transsexual process and found a deeper sense of wholeness and inner harmony; and the parents of gay sons and daughters who, like me, are still learning how to love a little better.

Together we keep trying to practice the kind of love Jesus of Nazareth had in mind when He invited us to love one another as He loves us. Some days we manage it beautifully; other days we are still practicing.

I also wish to express my sincere gratitude to Rev. Dr. David Nash for his encouragement and support.

The Reverend Doctor James R. Black
Minister of Word and Sacrament
Certified Chaplain
Insured Therapist

Table of Contents

Introduction

This short, easy-to-read essay offers much-needed and helpful information to the general public, especially thinking Christians, congregations, gay persons, and their family members. This book invites all of us to gain more understanding of what more mature adults are like on this sometimes, uncomfortable topic.

I do not intend to "cover this subject" as much as you may have wanted or expected. This is because it is an extremely complicated, multilayered subject, and it does demand far more than I am offering. Still, by gaining more good understanding, all of us may have less bias and be more compassionate with one another, gay-wise, race-wise, and with less xenophobia, fear of other cultures.

Most studies on this subject offer no concrete and or final "causation" as to why anyone is who or as they are. All of us are products of chromosomes, environmental, and socialization influences. Recently, more in the medical field believe that there is chromosomal causation. Each "category" has his or her, for discussion purposes, obligation to be responsible toward others, regardless of gender and or emotional or orientation preferences.

Many have no power over what life gave them, race, LGBTQI persons, being Jewish, "straight," birth defects, and so on. However, some behaviors can be chosen. We have the power not to be or act out simply because of who we are. The emphasis in this book is for all to be more appropriate and responsible for who or what we are, and to take responsibility for the rewards, benefits, and or costs and losses that come with our choices.

The mature LGBTQI persons I know are fine, responsible people. There is so much more to them than their orientation. They appreciate anyone who has no regard for their orientation but appreciates them for being so much more than any label far too many, unfortunately, place on them. I, personally, have been put off for being a white Anglo-Saxon male.

As a minister, you need to be prepared for me to use my "Reformed" faith tradition to enter into this challenging subject. Also, I will be the first to say that, like many of you, I do not "know it all." In fact, I welcome your input and wish we were close enough to share in good conversation, where I could hear your solid arguments and, most likely, would agree with you. I invite you to have your own good thoughts and ideas about any of the following.

Ours is a moral universe. Like a wall, we have the freedom to run into it if we like, but in time, we only hurt ourselves. My God sends no one to hell, but He weeps as He watches so many of us choose to go there on our own.

My definition of "heaven" and "hell" may not be yours. Yes, I see all good coming from the One Christians call the "Cosmic Christ," who earned this right by His sacrifice. He received this title only after His resurrection. Many followers call Him their "Savior," but far more Christians need to see Him as their "Lord," loving others as much as they can, as He did. "Hell" is simply where godly love is absent.

Too many of us, gay and or straight, often look at the "other" as being "all alike." This is absurd. No two people are alike, even identical twins, one of whom I am. The fact is that each of us is not just like the person we were ten years ago, gay or straight. My hope is that we will see each other as individuals and accept a person on the basis of character and compassion.

My hope is that each of us can put reins on our egos and listen to one another.

"Ah, but a man's reach should exceed his grasp, or what's a heaven for?" — Robert Browning

 I came across some earthy wisdom the other day. "Trying to reason with some people with closed minds is like a bee trying to convince a fly that honey is so much better than poo-poo" (Anon). Sane, sensible adult people listen.

Christianity seems to have two major groups. One group emphasizes compassion, acceptance, and lifting people up who are down. Jesus is their model for living. Everyone is made in the image of God. Christians are invited to love everyone God loves. Labels are rarely kind things to place on anyone.

The other group of Christians believe in law and order, a kind of "the way things are and behavior ought to be." My book may not be a favorite of the "law and order" type who think that this or that person should always be "this or that way." Whenever we divide and judge, others may be labeled as "less than." Doing this invites dehumanization to raise its ugly head.

I would hope that all of us would exhibit more compassion, watch our labeling, and lift others up as persons, each with one's own individuality, so that labels might disappear. I must quickly add that both Christian groups have their place. Jesus said that we are to be "as wise as serpents and as gentle as doves" (Matthew 10:16). Each of us has to decide which way we should "lean" when it comes to many issues in life.

Our world runs on politics, the military, economics, and ideologies. The first three, like science, are hard, foundational, and structural. However, what is needed is the best ideology that can be had. This is the emotional power at work that can determine the other three. We have chosen democracy. Yet there are other emotional, ideological powers at play that, unless kept within certain boundaries, can be the earth's total undoing.

In the midst of all these emotional powers at work around us, I stand, get recognized, and make a motion. "People of the world, I nominate the Judaic-Christian ideology as the primary ideology of our day. Can I get a second to this motion?"

Did you know that "the pursuit of happiness" means being able to keep learning?

I know several "queer," the generally accepted term for the twenty-three-plus categories of persons, Christians who are ministers in several denominations doing excellent work. Their congregations do not care how much they know but yearn to know how much they care. I also join them in hoping that the day will come when, like racism, this entire topic will fade away from even being worthy of conversation.

With much respect and appreciation, I dedicate this book to you, the reader, whether "gay" or "straight," whatever those mean, as many of us have our own private weaknesses. I also dedicate it to my two adopted children, especially to the bisexual and lesbian women in my faqmily, whom I love and admire for all the good work they are now doing for so many others. Ashley has added much to the writing of this book. I am indebted to persons within the book title. It is only natural and respectful that I invited them to assist me in this essay.

"Two things fill the mind with ever new and
increasing wonder and awe…
the starry heavens above me and the moral law
within me."
— Immanuel Kant

Let us begin with both.

PART I:

FOUNDATIONS

Science and Faith
"Christianity and Trust"

"Speaking for the motion above, I am intentionally entering into some 'theology' with you to 'set the stage' and invite you to join with me in learning how to 'change for the better' and not remain 'blocked' in our various biases concerning racism and psychosexual differences. Being a minister, it is easy for me to 'slip' into coming across as a bit 'preachy' and or 'teachy'. Bear with me and, hopefully, the book will prove to be worth your patience and whatever you may have had to pay to buy it."

Scientists have strongly claimed that creation began about thirteen and a half billion years ago. If so, there was no "bang," because sound requires an atmosphere through which sound can travel. But since the discovery of a visiting comet from outside our solar system, 3I/ATLAS, astrophysicists are now forced to question much of the "truth" that science assured us of earlier. The point is this: we all must stay open to learning, "happiness," above, new and better things from both science and faith communities.

Child: "Where is God, Mommy?"
Mom: "God is everywhere, honey."
Child: "I don't want God just to be everywhere, just somewhere!"

My brother-in-law, Dr. Lawrence Gurley, was a research specialist at America's scientific think tank in Los Alamos, New Mexico, the National Institute of Science. He, like most high-level scientists, tolerated the presence of Christianity for many years. He lectured and wrote about his acclaimed, accepted scientific theories. Later, however, he discovered that his ideas were just another "stepping stone" in the annals of science. That realization struck him. Even accepted scientific "truth" can be relative, as his theory was now passé.

Lawrence loved research. He even visited "sweat tents" with Native peoples about the work he was doing, part of which involved the genetic code, for years. He also spoke with religious leaders in India, worked with the natives of Haiti, and so on. Then, this Jesus story became fascinating to him. In fact, gulp, he became a person who highly respected Jesus of Nazareth and was profoundly impressed with His logic and "social programs."

Fellow scientists began to look at him kind of funny, but Lawrence could not have cared less. He had learned that there is so much more in this universe than most busy scientists had taken the time to consider. Our astrophysicists have just admitted that all their knowledge pales in comparison with what they have recently learned about physics from the passing 3I/ATLAS, which was being monitored by telescopes on Earth and beyond. Science, while tremendous, can have limitations and "miscues" itself.

Dr. Gurley became a Christian because some of its valuable thinking is more steadfast and time-tested. Yes, religion is not science, and science is not religion.

Science has to do with structure and substance, and "faith" has to do with meaning, purpose, emotions, and "being" itself. Each has its place in the scheme of things.

So, what is a "Christian"? A person who has reached a point where they trust a person named Jesus. In fact, they have bet both their life and their death on Him being their Lord and Savior. Granted, it usually takes a lot of living and time for a person to "feel this" and be serious about this profession. Also granted, most so-called "Christians" really are not. But before I get off my point, it takes great "trust" to reach this position. To me, "faith" is not irrational. It is simply "reason grown courageous."

What is "trust"? If you are like me, I need to know three things about anyone before I place trust in them. Does this person have good character? Is this person competent? Have I had enough meaningful contact with this person for me to place my trust in him or her? Christians, the true ones, feel that Jesus offers the best answers to life's largest questions. Questions like, "Is there a God?" "How does God feel about humans?" "Why was I born," that is, "do I have some purpose in this universe?" "How can I best live my life and face my own death?"

All big stuff, huh? Is all of life merely "relative," or part of something far larger or grander than what I have either taken for granted or not even stopped to think much about at all? They "trust" because they know the "character" of this Man, they know He is "competent" to do what He says He can, and they have had a great deal of "connection" with Him through Scripture and fellowship with others who exhibit His presence in and through them.

I mean, you, dear reader, will be fortunate enough to be able to die. Think about it. Of all the sperm that raced toward that one egg at that moment in its existence, yours beat out all the other millions that failed to enter. None of those other millions will ever know human life with its oceans, mountains, music, friends, good food, and making love, and so on.

So where are we at this point? This Christian author believes in science and believes that the Creator, who is always beyond our full understanding, has entered into a tiny mudball called "Earth," possibly other planets too, with intelligent life as well. Each of us is merely a living, breathing piece of stardust. The next sentence will tell you that you are about to enter into "the big league."

In the Gospel of John, the Greek reading of that passage says that "God so loves," present tense, the "cosmos," Greek for "universe," that He gave us His only begotten Son, that whosoever takes Him seriously will have everlasting life (John 3:16). It means that at our birth, we have life and, at our death, more and better life. Any who believe this can feel that they are "cured," and not just healed, that is, at peace with how they can live a meaningful life and enter into their own death. Yes, it may take a lifetime before one reaches this very personal emotional and psychological state.

Jesus did say, "I came that you may have life and have it more abundantly" (John 10:10). This means, "filled to the top and running down the sides."

Commitment to this Jesus who, after His resurrection, became, for Christians, the "Cosmic Christ," matters deeply. Thinking Christians are reasonable people who "buy into" this story, "trust" Him, and intentionally want to say, "Thank You, Creator God, for giving us not just life, but the opportunity of a good one, full of a living hope." They are the ones who have dropped their old ways of thinking and their egoism and are giving themselves over to this Cosmic Christ, hook, line, and sinker, doing so gratefully and showing it with commitment.

They call this Cosmic Christ not just their "Savior," but "Lord," trying to thank Him as they can with their own lives and the living of them. These are called "Christians." They are "weird" enough to believe in a resurrection, something many think is silly, even though, ironically, while refusing to believe it, they sure hope it is true.

Again, "faith" is simply "reason grown courageous." As such, a Christian's "faith" is not illogical or irrational. There is a historical basis for it and a massive amount of personal experience behind deep "faith." We are not just after "life after death." That is selfish and shallow. It is about a quality of relationship with God and with others who are "in Him" and "in one another," the pure with the pure, meeting.

It is then that all God started will be completed and fulfilled. Hey, you come too.

Are Christians really better than others? No. All they try to do is tell and demonstrate to those who are "hungry" in so many ways where there, by grace, is "bread." Re-read this last sentence. We are just men and women who feel, for good reasons, that we are on the "right road," going in the "right direction" with our lives and with the living and dying of them because of the Man from Nazareth.

For thousands of years, humans have tried to reach up and appease some god or other with dances, sacrifices, and so on, hoping their crops will grow and their battles will be won. Christmas, to Christians, is God saying, "No need for all of that. I am coming to reach you." It seems that God came out of His own kind of time and space and "splashed" down among us.

Most Christians are not dummies. They simply take this Christ story seriously and love it. They find hope in it, meaning in it, "the" answer to the God question, but they know that all of this is not over yet. After all, Jesus told the Apostle Peter to get over his own ideas of the way Messiahs are supposed to act and to "get in line right behind" Jesus, the Drum Major, and that, in His own time and way, He will lead those who are behind Him to where He is going and wants to take us, too.

Robert Frost's poem, "The Pasture," reads, "You come, too." This is what Jesus is saying to Peter and to the rest of us. You come, too.

Before we move forward, let's pause a moment.
Science asks how the universe works.
Faith asks why it matters.

Most of us are still learning the answers to both.

Introduction into "Queer"

"All behavior is motivated by something" (2). All the way from the humble amoeba up to the human species. The author is limiting this book to only a few of the various major forms of sexual behaviors and expressions. As I wrote earlier, this is a very complicated field, with multiple layers of complexity. Personally, it is difficult for me to understand and explain some categories, such as bisexual, polysexual, nonsexual, the field of cross-dressers, queen and king drag performers, fetishes, and so on. They, too, are motivated and have either psychological and or purely biological reasons for their behavior.

To my knowledge, the total number in each category appears to be small when compared with the entire population. A recent Gallup poll states that in 2024, about 9.3 percent of the 345 million Americans are in this broad category (Wikipedia). This means that almost one person in ten you meet is part of the "queer" community. To my knowledge, none are unworthy of respect or dignity, nor are they unworthy of God's love.

Christ's death on the cross shows the length God is willing to go to have a right relationship with humanity, and the benefits of this include and invite all human beings into a profound relationship with God. However, it is effective only when this kind of love is understood and accepted by a person. Then, this love is also totally and existentially mutual.

To Christians, "queer" persons are "one in the Spirit, one in the Lord," and no one, no one, is "less than" or "second to" God, who saw all of us "queer" in the areas of holiness and purity due to our being caught up in Sin, with a capital "S."

"What is the sound of one hand clapping?" (A Japanese Zen koan) (3). The answer is, there is no sound. It takes two. And so it is with humanity and God. Together, we can still turn this old, hairy-chested, fang-and-claw, I-got-mine-now-you-get-yours kind of world we live in around.

This book is for adult adults and for those who hope to become one. Science is fundamentally about the substance and structure of life, and Judeo-Christian spirituality has to do with the meaning and purpose of life and how one is to live.

"Judge not according to appearance, but judge righteous judgment."
— John 7:24

Understanding almost always begins when judgment pauses.

PART II

SCRIPTURE, IDENTITY, AND HUMAN DIGNITY

I'M GETTING TO THE LGBTQ, ETC. PART

In the Gospel of Luke, there are three parables of interest to this LGBTQ topic: the Parable of the Prodigal Son, the Lost Sheep, and the Lost Coin. The first is a picture of two men: one who left home, much like those who have left the church, often called "Dones," and another who remains yet is self-righteous, judging others as holier than thou. The second parable is about a sheep that wandered away from the flock, but the Good Shepherd left the ninety-nine, wow, just to track down the one who wandered from the congregation. The third parable tells of a coin that a widow depended upon for survival. The coin knew nothing, much like many folks who are simply living as they can: eating, sleeping, and reproducing without deeper reflection. Even a dog can do that.

You are right. It is not just some LGBTQ folks who are like this, but an entire array of persons and professions who are the same way. We are all sinners, and there are few who can doubt this. At this time, however, I am focusing on my desire to promote and call for the dignity and rights of those who are treated as outcasts or viewed as 'less than' so unfairly by others. Their loved ones and parents are hurt, too. This book is for them and their parents, to read, rest, and to encourage others they know who may have concerns.

Me? I am far from perfect myself. I am disliked by many for my views, too. I am 'straight,' whatever that means, but I know that, deep down, I have lived a life that is often unworthy when compared with the profession I am in as a minister. I know, personally, many gay persons whose lives are lived far more 'righteously' than my own. By the way, 'righteous' means 'pure' or 'holy.' This has to do with mindset and motives.

If you have ever been to an A.A. or N.A. meeting, you will see many people doing what they can to become 'clean' again. Each of us is 'dirty' in some ways. Yet every time an old alcoholic or addict comes back, even for the tenth time, everyone there applauds and welcomes him or her with open arms. Why? Because they know that none of us is 'pure,' 'clean,' or entirely 'right.' We usually cannot heal ourselves. It often involves the love and understanding of others to become 'cleaner,' 'better,' more 'light-like' rather than dark. No one accomplishes this fully in this life but, by golly, we all can keep trying. So we keep accepting and encouraging one another, welcoming one another. We want to be more 'light-like.' So we at least do what we can to stop, restrain, or cut down on our weaknesses. As we do this, Christian or not, we know we are still loved and wanted. Christians know that God has always loved all of us and is pulling for us as we continue to try to become more 'light.' This is why church dropouts or newcomers are warmly welcomed and rejoiced over when they come through that church door, or should be. As long as all of us keep trying, stopping or restraining what harms ourselves and others, we are 'in.'

As for the data or demographics of these groups or categories, I will refer you to various surveys regarding 'types' and 'numbers' in relationship to the entire population. As you might imagine, there are major trends based upon age groups reporting. This is because older persons have not been as open or willing to report on themselves, while younger persons are more open these days. Most surveys indicate that the majority within these combined communities identify as 'bi,' followed by gay males, with lesbians third, though many prefer the word "queer" rather than "lesbian," and trans persons representing smaller percentages than the groups above. I leave it to your curiosity to explore where each group stands in terms of percentages within society as a whole. As an addendum, the percentage of gay and lesbian persons in the priesthood and convents has been reported as higher in the Roman Catholic Church than in the general population, according to various sources. Granted, this last group is more 'celibate' than most, not all, of the others above.

And by the way, what I share here is the view of this one Christian. I do not speak for others. What I share here will not be agreed with by all Christians or LGBTQ persons. Being human myself, I remain open to listen, learn, and grow, and I hope that you, the reader, are this way, too.

MY CREDIBILITY

Aside from what is on the cover of my book, you can read my biography. I worked on a Gender Reassignment Team at Methodist Hospital in Jacksonville, Florida, counseled and traveled with members of this large community, worked with staff members of this national and worldwide community, and have family members who are part of this broad community. Oh, I am also a certified and insured Marriage and Family Therapist, now retired. I will share words below from members of the LGBTQ community here and there. Much of this book and its focus has been influenced by my conversations with many such persons. I have them to thank for much that is shared herein.

You will notice that I do not offer insights into all members of this community, only some. Why? Because there are about twenty-three categories, and few are aware of these or of what is unique about each. I invite you to become familiar with them and how they are defined simply by asking "Siri." She can give you time to investigate each category and its uniqueness. You may also search the web and review information on Wikipedia.

My sole thrust is to promote dignity, respect, greater understanding, and to always exhibit kindness toward each and every person. Why? Because my faith tells me that each is made in the Image of God, capable of a divine relationship with God, and that Christ is in the "love business," desiring His kind of love to dwell within us and be shared with others. All of us are invited to understand this, to practice it, and to build one another up in love.

Some bisexual persons jokingly claim that they love everyone already. They know this "ability" is not the same kind of love Jesus is speaking about. The love Jesus describes can be seen in the Parable of the Good Samaritan, Luke 10:25–37. "Samaritan" was a dirty word to the Jews in Jesus' earthly days. Yet this man saw a legitimate need and went out of his way for someone who hated him. It cost him time and money, and he took a risk, simply because this beaten man needed help and deserved attention. Each of us is called to do likewise. His love will always cost those who try to follow Him and repeat His will and ways. You may be opposed, laughed at, imprisoned, lose money, spend time, and be misunderstood. As they say in New York, "figgetaboutit." We do what we can, but God carries the heavier load and protects His own. I sometimes refer to God as "She." God is Spirit and encompasses what we experience as both male and female within God's own being.

All of us have a calling. It is to know Him and to make Him known. Why? Because He has given us a way to live, as well as a why and a how. He invites us into a deep relationship with Him and, from that relationship, to become better to ourselves and others, and to bring joy to God's heart. We are to place God first and to show Christlike love to our neighbors as though that neighbor, whoever it may be, were our very own self. Yet each of us must come to know ourselves first and learn to love ourselves as Christ does, warts and all. No one does this perfectly in this life, but we are given the opportunity to do what we can. As we do, we feel valued, appreciated, wanted, and needed. We gain courage, vision, and hope. We may bear the Fruit of the Spirit and become candidates for the resurrection. Not a bad promise.

Permit me to digress a bit. It would be hard to imagine what the world would be like were it not for LGBTQ persons. Imagine the artwork, sculpture, music, plays, writing, and ballet that might not exist for those of us who love culture. One example is the English engineer Alan Turing, who deciphered the German Enigma machine code. Were it not for him, World War II might have continued far longer. Consider also entertainers such as Elton John. History records clergy, political leaders, artists, and countless others who have identified as gay. Many denominations here and overseas include gay clergy, some of whom are married.

Some have even suggested that David and Jonathan, Saul's son, shared a deeply intimate friendship, as did Ruth and Naomi. Whether or not these relationships were sexual, their closeness has been noted by many biblical scholars. Again, you may consult available resources to discover the thousands of talented LGBTQ persons in politics, government, business, industry, and medicine, all of whom deserve gratitude for their contributions. Each does what he or she can to serve and influence others. It reflects something of goodness at work in and through us. It feels good. It feels healthy.

As for those who identify as unsure, some use language to describe uncertainty about where they fit within the broader community. They may love deeply and appropriately yet not experience strong sexual desire toward one sex or the other. Like all of us, whether gay or straight, feelings and understandings can shift over time.

A quick reminder:
learning something new rarely harms us.

Refusing to learn often does.

NATURE HERSELF
HAS GIVEN SUCH TO THE WORLD

Check me out on this. Listening to NPR two weeks ago, I heard a special on homosexuality in nature. It turns out that almost all primates, we being one of them, exhibit same-sex behavior within their species. Lower animals do as well. Think of your pets at home. Birds, reptiles, insects, and many other species display such behavior. These patterns have existed alongside humans since our earliest origins, some three to four hundred thousand years ago.

One's gender identity and emotional reactions are extremely complex topics. One example involves bisexual persons. Whether anatomically male or female, some experience profound attraction toward both sexes. This is not an easy world for them. In time, they may marry and appear to be in a heterosexual marriage. One partner may still experience strong emotional and sexual attraction toward the same or opposite sex. It may be in the best interest of the marriage for this reality to be known and honestly acknowledged. Still, it is the obligation of the bisexual partner, as with any highly sexual heterosexual partner, to remain faithful within the marriage. This is not easy, and both persons must recognize that acting out fantasies outside the marriage could not only be shallow but may lead to the end of the relationship.

Deep down, regardless of sexual stimulation, human beings cannot and should not live as compulsive, impulsive creatures, using others as objects. Some need help if they fall into patterns of using those around them. As I have said, it is extremely difficult to rise to a higher way of living, but in the long run, choosing the higher road reflects greater spiritual maturity. To date, therapy efforts aimed at changing sexual orientation have rarely been effective. Some attempt such change but, over time, often return to their previous orientation.

As for marriage, it existed long before the Bible came into being. Consider the Code of Hammurabi in ancient Babylon, which predates Abraham. Many ancient cultures recognized marriage long before biblical texts were written. I will not insult your intelligence by listing all the benefits of marriage for a couple and for society, nor the costs when such unions are prevented. Gay persons also have a right to a full life, as do heterosexual persons. Prior to the Supreme Court's decision permitting same-sex marriage, some heterosexuals jokingly asked, "Why don't they have the right to the same conflicts the rest of us have?" The reality is that many same-sex marriages experience struggles similar to those of heterosexual marriages.

There can be serious complications if a legally recognized marriage is later dismissed by changes in the law. If one spouse moves to another state and the other remains, and if either seeks a divorce, legal recognition can become complicated if the states involved do not equally recognize the marriage. These situations can create significant legal and personal challenges. At present, same-sex marriages are legally recognized nationwide. This recognition reduces many practical and legal difficulties and extends benefits long associated with marriage. Many believe they possess a constitutional right not only to life, but to liberty and the pursuit of happiness, including the freedom to enter a meaningful marital relationship. And yes, such marriages have struggles, as all marriages do. We are, all of us, still human. Personally, I think most marriages consist of two imperfect people who spend years learning how to live together with greater understanding and contentment.

In the mytho-historical story of Adam and Eve, Adam sees Eve and exclaims, "Wow." The Hebrew text suggests that Eve was formed from Adam's side. Whether one understands this account as literal history or theological narrative, the story speaks to enduring human truths. Many ancient cultures told creation stories and wrestled with the origin of evil. Even if one does not view Eden as a historical location, the truth conveyed in the story continues to describe the human condition. We are capable of rebellion and self-centeredness. Religious traditions speak of "sin" as a condition in which all of us participate. Some Jewish interpreters have suggested that the serpent represents human intelligence joined with free will. Adam and Eve chose wrongly in their desire to be like God. We continue to struggle with that same tendency today.

It is important for the reader to know that I also value science. I do not see the Bible as a scientific textbook, but as a vital guide for how to live and how to understand the spiritual dimension of life.

"God created humankind in His image…
male and female He created them."
— Genesis 1:27

Perhaps we have been reading
the words too narrowly.

Between what we name
and what God creates,
there may be more life
than we have yet allowed ourselves to see.

IN THE BIBLE, GENDER IS NOT BINARY.

The Bible employs many merisms, in which two contrasting words stand in for a whole spectrum. "Male and female" is one of them.

I'm not proud to admit it, but the first time I met a trans person, I felt awkward. It was 1999, and I was visiting my friend Jean in the hospital. Sitting up under a canvas of clean white sheets, she was telling me about a friend of hers who had recently transitioned from male to female. As if on cue, that friend appeared. Bounding with energy, she swept into the room. Tall and lanky, with long, curly, strawberry-blond hair, she wore jeans, a crisp white blouse with the top three buttons undone, a simple gold chain, and dangling gold earrings. "You look great," Jean pronounced from her hospital bed.

"Thanks," this beautiful woman beamed. "I didn't even get any strange looks on my way over here… but it was my first time riding a bicycle since the operation." Then she added a monosyllabic reflection on the experience: "Ouch." I had no idea how to respond, so I offered a small smile that I hoped would suggest support more than shock. The idea of someone undergoing gender confirmation surgery was new and almost alarming to me then.

My understanding of gender identities has expanded greatly in the intervening years. Reading books by transgender writers, especially Jennifer Finney Boylan's *She's Not There*, helped me to appreciate how hard it can be for trans people, and for queer people more broadly, to live into themselves. People who have the courage and support to claim their sexual orientation or gender identity often face discrimination, recrimination, and even criminalization. The violence done to queer people, especially those who are trans or nonbinary, can be physical, psychological, emotional, and spiritual.

Much of this violence could also be characterized as biblical, since it utilizes the Bible to justify harm. Many Christians believe that scripture sanctions the existence of just two, binary genders: male and female. Citing the Bible to justify their views, some Christians promote anti-queer beliefs, actions, and legislation that can have devastating and even deadly ramifications for trans and nonbinary people. In many churches, the Bible has been weaponized to deny basic human rights, like the right to safety.

Any biblical text can be understood on various levels and in multiple ways. An anti-queer biblical interpretation, like any other, stems from the reader's own presuppositions and biases interacting with a specific passage. Interpretations take root and have life when there is a community to adopt and share them. In this way, damaging interpretations of the Bible have been wielded against queer people through churches, often without any recognition that there are other ways to read these same texts.

The Bible's own genesis begins when God mythologically forms the universe in seven days, as told in Genesis 1:1–2:4a. Day one: light and dark, giving evening and morning (1:1–5); day two: the dome separating the waters above and below (1:6–8); day three: seas, dry land, and vegetation (1:9–13); day four: sun and moon (1:14–19); day five: birds and swarming sea creatures (1:20–23); day six: land animals and humans, both male and female (1:24–31). After all this labor, God wisely takes day seven for self-care and rest, since creation is complete (2:1–4a).

Much is missing from this account. Evening and morning have been formed, but is there no midday? The seas hold water, but where are the rivers, lakes, and marshes? The planets and stars are not mentioned, did God create them? What about amphibious creatures? Elements absent from the text are undeniably present in the world and integral to God's creation.

Instead of attempting an exhaustive catalog of everything in the universe, the writers instead offer a series of merisms. This literary device names two ends of a spectrum and implicitly includes all that lies in between. An example of a merism can be found today in traditional wedding vows when people pledge to stand by each other "for richer or for poorer." No one assumes the marriage should break up if their financial situation stays the same. Rather, the merism conveys totality by mentioning opposite parts to signal expansive inclusion.

The Bible employs merisms repeatedly. For example, the Israelites recurrently long for the land flowing with milk and honey (e.g., Exod. 3:8, 13:5; Lev. 20:24; Num. 13:27). These two foods can be read as a merism: that which spoils quickly and that which lasts indefinitely. In Psalm 139:2, the prayer affirming God's omniscience, "You know when I sit down and when I rise up," clearly suggests the Deity's awareness of all actions, not just these two. God's authoritative assertion as "the Alpha and the Omega" (Rev. 1:8, 21:6, 22:13) indicates not solely the first and last letters of the Greek alphabet but an all-encompassing power.

The creation of male and female (Gen. 1:26–27) can also be read as a merism, consistent with the rest of this account. On day six, God makes these distinct humans as ends of the gender spectrum. In between are the people with other identities: transgender, intersex, nonbinary, and all gender-expansive people. Recognition of this fullness may be why God speaks of creating humans "in *our* image" (Gen. 1:26, emphasis added), underscoring inclusion. The binary language of male and female doesn't appear until the following verse, establishing the polarity as another merism. God then pronounces this spectrum of human genders, along with the rest of this day's creation, as "very good" (Gen. 1:31).

The second creation myth that follows in Genesis 2 offers another possibility for gender inclusivity. As Phyllis Trible points out in her foundational study *God and the Rhetoric of Sexuality*, the person formed in this account is "sexually undifferentiated." The Hebrew word used to designate this original human is *ha-adam*, closely translated as "the earth creature" made from the *adamah*, or "earth." Another way to convey this pun in English is to translate *ha-adam* as "the human" from the *adamah*, "humus." While Hebrew nouns are gendered and the word *adam* is masculine, the grammatical form of this noun does not convey corporeal gender. Similarly, the word *behemah* in Hebrew is feminine and means "large animal," but obviously not all large animals are female.

Yet most readers presume that the first human created in this account is male because translators render *ha-adam* as "the man," imposing maleness on an ungendered human. Of the fifteen times the phrase *ha-adam* appears in the Hebrew of Genesis 2:7–25, the NRSV and NRSVue render it as "the man" thirteen times and "man" the other two. This translation not only magnifies maleness but reinforces the gender binary by linguistically erasing the possibility of a person who is nonbinary as our common mythological ancestor.

Granted, the writers of this ancient text likely had a male person in mind as the first human because they were men and perceived the world through their own physical bodies. Most people in the ancient world woke up every morning with the same goal: try not to die that day. Only the cultural elite had the time and resources to acquire expensive writing materials and the skills of literacy. They wrote about a powerful male God and a first human who mirrored themselves. And yet, biblical texts invite a wide range of interpretations that are sustained by a close reading of their original languages. The beginning of the Bible offers promising possibilities for exploring and affirming gender identities beyond the binary.

Perhaps eunuchs are the most obvious examples in the biblical world of people not limited by the gender binary. Jeremiah 41:16 separates eunuchs from males and females by listing soldiers, women, children, and eunuchs, signaling awareness of gender ambiguity that we might describe as nonbinary. Typically born male, a eunuch would become part of another gender category upon castration. Clearly, a trans or intersex person today is not the same as a eunuch in antiquity, nor can we assume that our standards of sexual identity are "normal" or "timeless," as scholars like Joseph Marschal, in *Intersex, Theology, and the Bible*, among others, have pointed out. Still, biblical eunuchs disrupt the binary categories that are often used to harm trans and intersex people.

The eunuch's gender ambiguity can also be seen in ancient Near Eastern iconography, notably neo-Assyrian bas-reliefs, in which eunuchs appear like women, with beardless faces, and like men, with wide-shouldered physiques. In her doctoral dissertation on eunuchs in the Bible and the wider ancient Near East, Janet Everhart points out, "As non-procreative males who are sometimes attractive sexual partners for both men and women, and sometimes celibate, eunuchs destabilize the binary concepts of both gender and sexuality." For this reason, I use the pronoun *they* when referring to any biblical eunuch.

Eunuchs appear with surprising frequency in the Hebrew Bible. They are mentioned forty-five times, often as court personnel with high rank. Their presence can be obscured in English since the Hebrew word for eunuch, *saris*, is repeatedly rendered in the NRSV as "official," "court official," and "officer." See, for example, Genesis 39:1, in which Potiphar, a *saris* of the Pharaoh, purchases enslaved Joseph. Potiphar's status as a eunuch helps to explain why Potiphar's wife lusts after handsome Joseph in the following verses. Additionally, translations of compound terms that suggest a eunuch in a position of authority remove the word *eunuch* entirely. In 2 Kings 18:17 and Jeremiah 39:3 and 39:13, the words *rab-saris*, which mean "great eunuch," are simply transliterated as "the Rab-saris" in the NRSV, a term devoid of meaning in English. Similarly, a key court official in the book of Daniel (1:3, 7, 8, 9, 10, 14, 18) is the *sar ha-sarisim*, "chief of the eunuchs." The NRSV translation of "palace master" erases the gender ambiguity of this respected person. Yet in other passages, both in Hebrew and in translation, the presence of a eunuch stands strong.

Jeremiah 38:1–13 tells the story of Ebed-Melech, a eunuch whose name translates to "Servant of the King." The prophet Jeremiah infuriates the king's advisers by urging the people of Jerusalem to submit to Babylon in the face of inevitable conquest (vv. 1–3). Seeing this counsel as tantamount to treason, the advisers, with the king's passive permission, throw Jeremiah into a muddy cistern (vv. 4–5). He is left there to die of dehydration, starvation, or suffocation as he sinks in the mud (v. 6). The mortal superhero who enters the scene to rescue the prophet is Ebed-Melech, an African eunuch from Cush, south of Egypt (v. 7). They leave the palace, where we infer they worked as a court official, and find the king at the gate to entreat him on Jeremiah's behalf (v. 8).

This eunuch has not only name, speech, action, and accessibility to the highest power in the land, but also what the king's lackeys lack: compassion. Ebed-Melech fearlessly condemns the advisers as having done evil in leaving Jeremiah to die (v. 9). Hearing the eunuch's appeal, the king immediately commands them to take three men to pull Jeremiah out of the cistern (v. 10). In Hebrew, this instruction specifies that Ebed-Melech should take three men "in his power" (*beyadcha*), a phrase omitted in English translation that further testifies to Ebed-Melech's status. Ebed-Melech gathers the necessary supplies, rags and worn clothes to place under the armpits, and instructs Jeremiah so he can be safely raised out of the cistern (vv. 12–13). Thanks to the eunuch, the prophet lives.

Acts 8:26–40 also tells of a respected eunuch from Africa. While not named in the text, the Ethiopian eunuch nonetheless has an impressive job description: they are the mighty ruler (Greek: *dunastes* from *dunamis*, meaning "power" or "force," like "dynamite") of the Ethiopian queen Candace's treasury (v. 27). After worshiping in Jerusalem, the eunuch is returning home, riding in their chariot and reading the scroll of Isaiah (v. 28). The acts of riding and reading attest to their wealth and erudition. Instructed by the Spirit, the apostle Philip approaches the eunuch and offers to interpret the passage they are reading, known to us as Isaiah 53:7–8 (vv. 29–33). These verses describe the "suffering servant," a figure who endures pain and even dies for the sake of others.

The eunuch respectfully asks, "I pray of you, about whom does the prophet say this, himself or about another one?" (translation mine). This same question has stymied Hebrew Bible scholars for centuries. But Philip is quick to answer with the convictions of a Jesus follower, proclaiming the gospel of Christ. Hearing this testimony, the eunuch acts as an exemplar of faith and asks Philip to baptize them when they encounter water. Philip does so before being "snatched away" by the Spirit (v. 39). The episode ends with the eunuch rejoicing, inferably feeling fully accepted as a baptized believer in Christ (v. 39).

Queer biblical interpretation plays with imaginative possibilities in the text, destabilizing conventional expectations to yield fresh readings. We might therefore envision the Ethiopian eunuch continuing the study of their scroll as the chariot proceeds and soon discovering the passage we know as Isaiah 56:3–5. In those verses, God affirms eunuchs: "Let not the eunuch say, 'Look, I am a withered tree'" (56:3b, translation mine). We might imagine the voice of the Lord thus encouraging our Ethiopian eunuch, averring that they are judged by the same standards as everyone else: keeping the sabbath, pleasing God, and maintaining God's covenant (v. 4). Their fidelity to God will be rewarded: "I will give in my house and my walls, power and a name better than sons and daughters" (v. 5a, translation mine). While the NRSV says that the eunuch will receive a "monument," the Hebrew word *yad* usually means "hand" or "power." A eunuch having power in YHWH's house is consistent with the recurring role of eunuchs as court officials, in this case with God as the divine monarch. Isaiah's prophetic blessing ends with a promise of perpetuity for the eunuch: "I will give them an everlasting name that shall not be cut off" (v. 5b).

Jesus, who knew the scroll of Isaiah (see Mark 7:6; Luke 4:16–21), was likely familiar with this blessing for eunuchs. The most concentrated reference to eunuchs in the Bible comes from Jesus' lips in Matthew 19:12. Jesus is teaching about interpersonal relationships and naming people of various sexual and gender identities: divorced women (vv. 1–8), adulterous men (v. 9), celibate people (vv. 10–11), eunuchs (v. 12), and children (vv. 13–15). His understanding of eunuchs is bolder in Greek than in English. A close translation renders verse 12a as follows: "For there are eunuchs who, out of their mother's womb, were born that way." Might Jesus be aware of congenital eunuchs or babies with ambiguous genitalia? He then acknowledges that most eunuchs have experienced castration: "And there are eunuchs who have been made eunuchs by others, and there are eunuchs who have made themselves eunuchs for the sake of the kingdom of heaven" (v. 12b). In no way does Jesus condemn eunuchs, people who transcend the limits of the gender binary. Rather, he acknowledges them as part of God's realm, then adds this final exhortation: "Let anyone accept this who can" (v. 12c).

Two thousand years later, Jesus' call to accept all people in God's realm, including those who are trans, nonbinary, queer, intersex, and gender-expansive, remains urgent. To be a queer, trans, or nonbinary person can mean risking attack simply because of who you are in your God-imaged self.

This article ends the way it began, with a confession. I am a cisgender heterosexual woman in a long-term marriage to a cisgender heterosexual man, with two cisgender children, a son and a daughter. Our family portrait appears almost anachronistically conventional. I do not presume to speak for anyone in the queer community. Nonetheless, I have shared my readings of these biblical texts, hoping they might serve others who, like me, seek ways to affirm the goodness of scripture for all God's children and prevent its misuse. The efforts of those of us who are allies with our queer siblings will not always be perfect or land as we intend. Yet innocent people are being made to suffer due to toxic biblical interpretations, so we need to try.

Let anyone accept this who can.

Some stories in Scripture have been used like stones.

Sometimes they were meant to be mirrors.

A REVISIT TO SODOM AND GOMORRAH

This very early story in what Christians call the Old Testament, well, you already know much about it. I will refresh your memory and add one more interpretation.

First, as you know, the "law of the desert" at that time required that any traveler be welcomed into a home and protected by the host of that residence. It was an extremely valued law, and woe unto him or her who failed to comply. Soon, three strangers, possibly "angels," arrive. That law is being honored. The townsmen hear of it and come to confront the host and the three visitors. The host offers his daughter to them for their violent desires, "Gee, thanks, Dad." They insist that the three strangers are to be their target and refuse the offer of the daughter. The story does not fully describe the outcome of the confrontation, but the threat itself is clear.

Second, we come to what many have called the "real" sin. Most Christians, particularly in more recent centuries, have assumed that the central issue was a homosexual act, and history has made a major issue of this interpretation, often using it to cause great and unnecessary harm to homosexual persons. Yet notice in the story that the host offered his daughter to men whom he presumed to be heterosexual. These men were acting violently and abusively. If they were heterosexual, their assault against male strangers was not an expression of loving relationship but of domination and humiliation. Even if the men had been homosexual, the intended attack would still have been sinful because it treated the guests as objects rather than persons. The sin in the story is attempted violence and degradation.

Such imbalance has tragically occurred in wartime and in certain penal institutions, where sexual assault becomes a tool of power.

What can we assume from this account? That gay persons are naturally evil? No. That God's creation reflects diversity? Many would say yes. Some of my rabbi friends have suggested that homosexuality is one more consequence of living in a fallen world, much like other human conditions. Others question that conclusion. Jesus Himself addressed suffering in John 9:1–17, making clear that blindness was not necessarily the result of personal or parental sin. Many physicians suggest that sexual orientation may involve complex factors during gestation and development. To what degree biological variation influences later behavior and desire remains a subject of ongoing research and debate.

The bottom line is this: some differences may not be matters of conscious choice. One of the gay organists in a church I served once told me, "Do you think I would choose to be gay? There are so many jokes and putdowns I have had to endure. It is unfair. I do not laugh at others for being born heterosexual." Another homosexual pastor said to a group of ministers, "Yes, I am gay, and I did not choose this. If I ever had a daughter, I would pray she would not have to endure the foul language and threats I have faced. Who would choose that?"

Fortunately, older generations of gay persons often faced harsher treatment than many do today, though prejudice has not disappeared.

Can you feel the hurt and pain some have endured simply because, for whatever reason, they discovered early in life that they were different? Some recognize their identity in childhood, including those who later identify as transgender. Others come to awareness during puberty. It can be deeply confusing and frightening for young LGBTQ persons.

How they respond to this reality, what decisions they make, and how they choose to live from that point forward remain matters of personal responsibility and moral discernment, for good or ill.

Time for a brief pause.

Every good conversation needs one.

Stretch your legs. The discussion continues.

PART III:

Relationships, Responsibility, and Love

TIME OUT FOR BASIC INFORMATION THAT ALL OF US CAN USE

1. The entire world needs three fundamental things: peace, bread, and healthy diversion. As we work for peace in as many ways and with as many constructive methods as we can, more resources become available for housing, education, health care, and related needs. Any remaining resources may be used for various kinds of entertainment and enjoyment.

2. Yes, AI is advancing quickly. Jobs are likely to remain in three broad categories. Level One positions may include nursing, data processing, military service, government work, and technical roles in medical, industrial, and manufacturing sectors. These are specialized positions that support and maintain a post-industrial society. Level Two roles, which may offer more modest compensation, include social sciences, counseling, teaching, social work, hospital support, and skilled trades such as plumbing and electrical work. Level Three jobs may include food service, various forms of labor, caregiving, and support assistance. These examples are not exhaustive, but they illustrate fields that are less likely to be fully replaced by AI.

3. We often speak of three broad economic groups in society: the "have-nots," the "haves," and the "have-mores." We also see divisions in outlook. Some pursue greater control, wealth, and power, while others emphasize freedom, access to truth, and health. These tensions shape much of our public life.

4. Support for LGBTQ Rights Holds Steady for Most, but Not All, Americans

Five Takeaways from PRRI's Latest Report

For more than a decade, PRRI has been tracking American attitudes about nondiscrimination protections for LGBTQ individuals, religiously based service refusals, and same-sex marriage. In our latest report, we find that while solid majorities of Americans continue to support nondiscrimination protections and same-sex marriage rights, support has dropped slightly over the past three years. Similarly, Americans' opposition to allowing small business owners to refuse service to gay or lesbian customers on religious grounds fell from 66% in 2022 to 59% this past year.

Here are my five major takeaways from our latest report.

a.) More than 7 in 10 Americans support LGBTQ nondiscrimination protections, including most people of faith.

Since 2015, PRRI has polled Americans on laws protecting LGBTQ individuals in jobs, housing, and public accommodations. Support has remained stable, moving from 71% in 2015 to 72% last year. Majorities in nearly every faith group support these protections, ranging from 54% of white evangelical Protestants to 92% of Unitarian Universalists, with Jehovah's Witnesses being the only exception. While support peaked among most groups several years ago, white Christians have seen the most notable decline in the past three years, from 76% in 2022 to 66% in 2025.

b.) Declining support for LGBTQ nondiscrimination protections is largely driven by Republicans.

In recent years, conservative Republicans in state legislatures around the country, and the current Trump administration, have worked overtime to curtail the rights of transgender Americans. In the last days of the 2024 election cycle, the Trump campaign and other Republican candidates flooded the airwaves with ads featuring anti-trans rhetoric. In the past week, Trump demanded that any version of the SAVE Act, ostensibly designed to make elections more secure from voter fraud, that appears before him to sign include provisions targeting transgender athletes and children. This bill faces an uphill battle in the U.S. Senate.

The GOP's persistent emphasis on transgender issues has meaningfully shaped support downward among Republicans. In 2025, 56% of Republicans supported nondiscrimination protections, down from 66% just three years ago. At the same time, support for broad nondiscrimination protections has remained steady among Democrats. Given that white Christians make up roughly two in three Republicans, it is not hard to see how support among white Christians has dropped ten points since 2022.

c.) Support for same-sex marriage is higher today than a decade ago, though support has slipped since its peak in 2022; most people of faith continue to support marriage equality.

Support for same-sex marriage remains higher today than a decade ago, 65% in 2025 versus 53% in 2015, but public support peaked in 2022, when 69% of Americans supported marriage equality.

Partisan shifts tell a more nuanced story. Notably, Republican support for same-sex marriage has not declined in the past three years, but roughly half of Republicans continue to oppose it. While Democratic support for marriage equality remains robust, support among Independents has declined in the past three years, now standing at 69%, down four points from its 2022 peak of 73%.

It is worth bearing in mind, however, that marriage equality enjoys broad support among most people of faith, including more than two-thirds of Catholics, white mainline or non-evangelical Protestants, Hindus, Buddhists, Jews, and Unitarian Universalists.

d.) Young Republicans in recent years have trended far more socially conservative, helping to drive a broader decline in support among younger Americans for LGBTQ rights.

Contrary to the expectation that younger generations act as a moderating force, young Republicans have trended significantly more socially conservative in recent years, contributing to an overall decline in support for LGBTQ rights among younger Americans.

In 2015, 80% of Americans ages 18–29 supported nondiscrimination protections for LGBTQ Americans. Last year, that percentage declined to 70%. This shift is particularly surprising given that younger Americans are more likely to identify as LGBTQ and are more likely to have a close personal relationship with someone who is queer than older Americans.

The decline is primarily driven, however, by sharply falling support among young Republicans. Among Republicans ages 18–29, support for LGBTQ nondiscrimination protections dropped from 74% in 2015 to just 50% last year. As recently as 2020, two-thirds of young Republicans backed same-sex marriage; today, only 52% do. Meanwhile, support among young Democrats on these measures has remained steady or increased slightly.

e.) Americans' views on transgender rights reveal a paradox that may shape future elections.

American public opinion on transgender rights reveals a striking paradox: broad support for general protections, but hesitation regarding specific policies.

Recall that 72% of Americans support laws protecting LGBTQ individuals from discrimination in jobs, public accommodations, and housing.

We decided in our latest survey to see if support for transgender Americans, specifically, might yield less support among Americans. It does not. We find that 71% of Americans agree that transgender people deserve the same rights and protection as other Americans, although differences align along the usual partisan divides.

However, a clear disconnect emerges when the conversation shifts to one specific form of public accommodation for transgender Americans: access to public bathrooms. A decade ago, only about a third of Americans supported "bathroom bills" that required transgender individuals to use the bathrooms corresponding to their sex assigned at birth rather than their current gender identity. In recent years, however, such bills have gained traction, with 21 states, all under Republican control, having passed restrictive measures.

Whether the passage of such bills will continue in the coming years is uncertain. Clearly, Republican strategists believe their often misleading attacks on gender identity were a key factor in Kamala Harris's loss to Donald Trump in 2024, so there is motivation to keep transgender issues at the forefront of their political appeals. Yet critics of such bills note that this "transgender playbook" did not resonate in recent gubernatorial races, as voters appeared far more concerned about the economy and broader issues related to the state of democracy.

5. As for marriage relationships, they operate with similar ups and downs, harmony and challenges, whether gay or straight. All couples bring their own unique idiosyncrasies to intimacy and love. A dear friend once told me, "If you truly love someone in a healthy way, intimacy can be expressed in ways that are mutually agreed upon, so long as there is no physical or emotional harm." Conversations about expectations should occur before marriage and continue throughout it. When your full agenda cannot or should not be enacted, work within your partner's comfort and boundaries. Love makes room for this. Also remember that no one person is everything another person needs. By the second or third year of marriage, many couples must decide whether they will remain committed. Keep in mind that you may not appear perfect to your partner either. So show grace, practice flexibility, and rise above ego for the sake of their well-being. During seasons of stress, offer an extra measure of patience and kindness. At the same time, be attentive if you are consistently excluded from decisions that properly belong to both partners.

6. As for healthy interaction, here is a method that, if faithfully practiced, can strengthen a marriage:

    a.   Hear your partner's words and notice their actions. Then listen for the feelings beneath those words and actions. Finally, seek to understand the needs that gave rise to those feelings. Pay attention to tone and mood, whether sarcasm, bitterness, or frustration. A common danger for many, whether straight or gay, is interruption. Do not interrupt while they are sharing. Be a safe place into which they can pour their words. Do not minimize what they are expressing or rush to provide solutions unless they ask for your input. They understand their situation better than you do. Quick directives often make a person feel unheard or belittled. Reflect on this carefully, because ignoring it can damage a relationship.

    b.   Every few months, ask your partner how they would like to be loved, supported, respected, and cared for. This is how mature love behaves. Most partners deeply appreciate being asked. They can then express, in reasonable and honest ways, what helps them feel valued. Neither of you will perform perfectly, but effort matters. When your partner knows you are trying to meet their needs, affection and trust grow. In time, they should also ask the same of you.

A minister once told me,
"If you cannot laugh while learning,
you probably are not learning very well."

"DID YOU KNOW" BITS OF INFORMATION

1. Dr. Seward Hiltner of Princeton Theological Seminary once said to me, "You Southern boys are kind of strange." I wondered where he was going with this. He continued, "When you are with a girl, you do not mind going from '1 to 24,' but not '25.' In that way, you can still feel righteous while having your fun." He went on to say that his Lord would see such behavior very differently. "To me, Jesus would view even holding hands for the wrong reasons as morally worse than going to '25,' even engaging in intercourse before marriage, if done for the right reasons." His point was about motive. Is the other person a whole human being to you, or merely an object for your pleasure? That is something all of us, gay or straight, ought to consider. Otherwise, what we do may return later in the form of shame or guilt, unless one has no conscience at all. I still remember what my mother would say before any date: "Jim, do not do anything that will keep you from liking yourself."

2. Sometimes, to prompt reflection, when the topic of gays arises, I ask a group of men or women, "How do you feel when you see a very attractive woman or a very handsome man?" I then explain that gays are not so difficult to understand. "Lesbians may feel toward certain women the same way you men feel." Or to women, "Gay men may feel much as you do when you notice a handsome

man." Then I ask, somewhat playfully, "Is it possible that you men are lesbians in male bodies?" Or, "Is it possible that you women might be homosexual in female bodies?" The reactions are often strong, but the point becomes clear: sexual attraction itself is not mysterious. It is human. It is also fair to say that both gay and straight persons have preferences. Some individuals hold no sensual appeal at all. With others, a good conversation is enough. And under certain circumstances, attraction may deepen.

3. Bias, prejudice, and confusion can also exist within LGBTQ-plus communities. One group may feel superior to another or less compassionate toward others within the same broad umbrella. Each person, in any grouping, is invited to consider how Jesus sees them and what He desires for and from them. This leads directly into the heart of the following reflection.

4. I remember spending an afternoon with a husband-and-wife psychiatric team. They spoke about the deeper psychological dynamics of sexual intimacy. They agreed that, while orgasm has its place and can be a powerful motivator, much more is occurring between partners. In Scripture, God instructs humanity to multiply and increase in number, Genesis 1:28. Few seem reluctant to attempt fulfilling that command. Yet intimacy involves more than biology.

This medical couple suggested that, in such moments, the child within each of us is also present. Human beings long to be held, to feel connected, safe, warm, and valued. We desire to matter to someone else. We do not want to feel alone, empty, isolated, abandoned, or vulnerable.

At the center of Christianity
is not a rulebook
but a person.

JESUS IS A "SOUL" MAN!

In the story of Jesus meeting the woman at the well, John 4:1–42, we discover just how well Jesus understands the human heart. We also see how close He is willing to come, how personally He engages us. Notice that Jesus steps across deeply embedded cultural habits and traditions. He meets the woman alone. As a rabbi, He was not expected to address a woman or ask anything of her, yet He does. Race, gender, and tradition, while historically understandable, carry spiritual limitations that Christ intentionally breaks through in order to make Himself known and received. His disciples are shocked, and so is the woman.

Their conversation moves beyond geography and worship locations to her deepest hunger and longing for body-and-soul satisfaction. Jesus reveals His knowledge of her life by referring to her five husbands. The discussion of "water" unfolds on two levels: satisfying physical thirst and addressing the deeper starvation for genuine fulfillment. Physical relationships alone have not satisfied her deepest needs. Who says Jesus does not know us or is unwilling to meet us where we are? Nonsense. Jesus cares deeply about the soul.

She responds, "Sir, give me this living water." In that encounter, she experiences profound hope and a renewed sense of worth. Something within her is touched at a deep level through that spiritual exchange.

God sees sexuality as good when expressed with the right person, in the right way, and at the right time. God leaves it to us to choose wisely so that intimacy results in what is good and life-giving for all involved. Without such discernment, people, bisexual or heterosexual, can reduce themselves to mere instinct rather than relational maturity.

You may ask, "How can anyone be expected to live at that level of goodness?" I know I cannot do so perfectly. Perhaps some celibate individuals, monks, priests, or those who identify as asexual, testify to a different experience of desire. Such persons may not feel strong sexual attraction yet are capable of deep emotional intimacy. Christians affirm that Jesus was fully human. It is not unreasonable to assume that He experienced natural human impulses. Yet He chose not to act on every impulse. Martin Luther once said, "You cannot keep birds from flying over your head, but you can keep them from building a nest in your hair." Again, it comes down to choice. I once had a Roman Catholic nun tell me she believed it was likely that Jesus masturbated. As a Calvinist, I was stunned! Wet dreams, maybe—that part of being human has nothing to do with morals, or the lack thereof.

Trans persons are not all that unique. Without any malevolent or disrespectful intent on my part, one might say that God engaged in a profoundly unique act of self-giving. In Paul's letter to the Philippians 2:5–9, we are told that "He emptied Himself and took on the form of a servant, being made in human likeness." In that sense, Christians affirm that God knows what it is like to live in a human body.

If God truly became human,
then nothing human
is completely foreign to Him.

JESUS IS A VERY REAL AND UNDERSTANDING PERSON

At this point, I find it helpful to speak of the beauty and goodness of Alcoholics Anonymous and Narcotics Anonymous. These are communities of persons struggling against alcohol and illegal drugs that have overtaken them physically and spiritually. For one reason or another, they slipped into addiction through a series of choices and vulnerabilities. Once inside that struggle, addicts will tell you that escaping is not easy, for emotional and chemically induced reasons. The body's normal endorphin systems can be disrupted, and substances begin to take their place. Over time, the body demands what has become the addiction.

What I love about A.A. and N.A. is this: if someone returns to a meeting, even for the fiftieth time, members stand, applaud, and welcome that person with love and open arms. There is no shaming, no condemnation, but a generous measure of grace. Why? Because that returning person is brave or desperate enough to keep trying. The effort itself is honored. What is so powerful about this?

Jesus tells us to love others. What does that mean, and is it even possible? To love does not mean that you must like everyone. That would be psychologically unrealistic, and Jesus understands that. To love means to care about another person's well-being and to desire that he or she receive what is due to every human being: food, shelter, opportunity, medical care, clothing, education, and dignity. Loving may cost the caregiver something. It may require giving money wisely, offering time, or risking being labeled sentimental or overly soft-hearted. Love is not cheap.

The same applies to trying to live as a Christian. None of us does it perfectly. After His resurrection, when Jesus stood on the shore of Galilee, He instructed the disciples to cast their nets on the other side of the boat, John 21:15. Later, He asked Peter three times whether Peter loved Him. The first two times, Jesus used a word for love that implied total self-giving and surrender. Peter responded that he loved Jesus as best he could, in the way of a devoted friend. Each time he answered honestly, "as much as I can." The third time, Jesus met Peter at Peter's level and asked him in the language Peter had been using. Peter was grieved, yet Jesus did not shame or accuse him. He accepted Peter where he was and invited him to continue loving Him in the best way Peter knew how.

That is a relief for all of us. We can only love according to our present understanding and capacity. Jesus knows we are not perfect. We are not invited to perfection, but to faithfulness in doing the best we can. The pressure to love flawlessly would crush us, and it is not what is asked.

This is why A.A. and N.A. celebrate and welcome those who return. They are doing the best they can in that moment. So are you and I, LGBTQ or not. We are invited not to strive merely to please Jesus or to avoid punishment, but to become healthier and more whole persons. In time, that wholeness blesses others as well. It is very practical.

Questions are good companions on the road to wisdom.

Answers sometimes arrive slowly.

Sometimes late, but they always arrive.

WHERE TO FROM HERE, LGBTQ-PLUS OR "STRAIGHT"?

All of us are sinners in one way or another, many in many ways. It makes little sense to create a hierarchy of sinners in the eyes of God. I know many straight, married persons who are far less loving toward their partners than some of the gay couples I know.

When I counsel couples who invite me to participate in their marriage preparation, even those previously divorced, I look for certain qualities.

a. Are they emotionally mature, and do they hold high intentions for themselves and for their partner?

b. Do they understand biblical love, and are they willing to practice it when infatuation fades and ordinary daily life begins?

c. What have they learned about themselves that will enable them to be a better partner? Patterns of thinking and behaving are often revealed by the observations of friends, family, or even the experience of a previous divorce. If there are skeletons in the closet, have they learned from them? Have they faced them honestly and allowed those hard lessons to mature them for the sake of their partner and others?

d. Do they intend to remain together in bad times and good, in sickness and in health, for better or worse? If one becomes bedridden and requires daily care, are they prepared for that level of commitment? Do they know how to disagree respectfully and resolve conflict with words? No one is ever to strike the other. If physical abuse occurs, the harmed partner should seek safety and take appropriate legal action, whether gay or straight.

e. We also discuss relationships with in-laws, shared goals, division of responsibilities in a fair manner, and the handling of finances, whether through one account or several accessible to both. For those considering children, we ask whether they agree on parenting philosophy and discipline. Finally, are they willing to participate meaningfully in a faith community they both can support?

"The kingdom of God is within you."
— Luke 17:21

PART IV:

THE KINGDOM PERSPECTIVE

SEEK YE FIRST THE KINGDOM OF GOD AND HIS RIGHTEOUSNESS, THEN...

Matthew 6:33

As a teenager applying for college, I was asked to write an idea that might positively impress the admissions committee. I quoted this verse. At the time, I assumed it meant that if I focused on heaven, I would eventually receive all the good things that produce a comfortable and stress-free life. I could not have been more mistaken.

Today, I understand the "Kingdom of Heaven" as a transformed way of seeing the world, a deeper and more enduring perspective on everything around me. It is not merely about future reward, but about a present reorientation of heart and mind. I am grateful to be part of that way of living. I have found peace.

The verse continues, "and all these things will be added unto you." What are these good things? For me, they include a way to live well and, when the time comes, a way to die well. Scripture speaks of the fruit of the Spirit, qualities that shape character and community. These spiritual and emotional gifts form a different kind of world within the world, one marked by love, joy, peace, patience, kindness, goodness, faithfulness, gentleness, and self-control. This is the atmosphere of the Kingdom. It is not an escape from reality but a renewed way of inhabiting it.

These benefits are not guarantees of wealth, physical healing, or social success. They do not remove every struggle. What they do provide is strength, resilience, and the capacity to restrain ourselves from harm. They give us courage to endure, to contribute meaningfully, and to know that our lives matter. Others may forget us in time, but God does not.

In this same world, there is also what many would call hell. Hell is where love is absent. It is where people wound one another, live in hardened self-interest, or cling to pride and indifference. I see hunger, homelessness, rejection, illness, injustice, and isolation. I also see those so insulated by wealth or status that they fail to notice suffering around them. That, too, is a kind of hell.

I once passed a rural sign advertising an estate sale that read, "Dead People's Stuff." It was blunt, even unsettling. It made me reflect on what truly endures. Have I lived in such a way that I have mattered before God?

When we step back from arguments,
something simple appears:
every human being is a neighbor.

A PARTIAL SUMMARY OF WHY LGBTQ-PLUS PERSONS ARE NEIGHBORS

1. God sees all of us as made in His image, capable of fellowship and worthy of dignity and respect.

2. No one is inherently better or worse than anyone else.

3. Many LGBTQ persons understand themselves to stand before God as they are, seeking to live responsibly and lovingly under the guidance of the Holy Spirit, just as any other believer does.

4. Many have accepted straight persons as brothers and sisters. We need and value one another for many reasons and in many ways.

5. Their talents, skills, and abilities have enriched culture, art, science, finance, politics, health care, education, and technology in countless ways.

6. They, too, seek the right to live full lives, free from fear, bondage, prejudice, hunger, and injustice, and with the security of life and liberty.

7. Along with Jews, persons of color, men and women, and all other groups, they share human and legal rights.

8. We all share the desire, and the declared right, to life, liberty, and the opportunity to learn, grow, and make a meaningful contribution to the world.

9. We share common humanity, common frailty, and the calling to live productively under both the order of nature and the will of God.

10. The story of Sodom and Gomorrah centers on violence, humiliation, and abuse, rather than loving, consensual relationships.

11. The modern term "homosexuality" does not appear in the original biblical texts. Later translations introduced terminology that continues to be debated among scholars.

12. Science does not yet fully understand the origins of sexual orientation, though research explores biological and developmental factors.

13. Christian homosexual and heterosexual citizens alike are called to love their neighbor as themselves.

14. Various Christian denominations have ordained gay clergy and continue to wrestle faithfully with these questions.

When I see egos laid aside, openness to listen and learn, and a willingness to step forward, often at personal cost, to help someone in need, those are my kind of people and, I believe, God's kind of people.

They understand love and are eager to share it with others, Jew or Gentile, rich or poor, white or person of color, gay or straight. These reflect the spirit of the Kingdom.

"You come, too." The invitation stands. As we walk this path of love, we discover more of its power, beauty, courage, and hope. We learn to allow Christ to determine who is "in" and who is "out."

Daily news reminds us of the consequences of failing to love. Yet the gospel speaks even more loudly of the good that lies ahead and extends its invitation again: "You come, too." Whoever seeks to think, feel, and act in this way, in gratitude for the One crucified and raised, is my brother or sister. The spirit of Christ is at work in many hearts, sometimes even beyond those who claim the name Christian yet fail to love well.

Those who live from this grace-filled center become the steady presence in the room. Their motives are shaped by a Christ-formed heart that continues to reach outward and say, "You come, too."

The older I get,
the more certain I become of two things:

God knows far more than I do,
and He is probably smiling at my attempts.

GOD IS BOTH "EVERYWHERE" AND "SOMEWHERE" ALL THE TIME, MOMMY

One great day, I will have to appear before my Creator. He will know how much of Himself there already is in me, and whether I have become part of the Trinity itself through the Holy Spirit within me. Every Christian bears something of the Trinity within. He may say to me, "Jim, all this talk and work you promoted to allow gays to marry, and all the concern you have shown for LGBTQ-plus persons having the right to freedom, justice, and a full life like all other persons, you were dead wrong. But come on in anyway. Your heart was in the right place."

"*You come, too.*"
— Robert Frost

The invitation remains open.

SURSUM CORDA. "L' HIYAM."

Up hearts. To life.

If you really and truly want deep peace and to become part of eternity itself, here are the keys. Meditate on them for a long time, and voilà.

Isaiah 26:3
Colossians 1:24–29
Matthew 6:33

CLOSING REMARKS

One final thought remains with me. I wish I had dug even deeper into explaining certain Greek words and the realities of Roman culture that shaped how scripture was first understood. Much of what many people believe today comes from misunderstandings that developed over time, as scripture was interpreted outside the context in which it was originally written. Even the writings of St. Paul have often been misread in our day. When those texts are carefully examined within their historical setting, a very different picture begins to emerge.

Seen in that light, it becomes painfully clear how easily modern assumptions have misled the public and steered many conversations in directions that have caused needless harm. Too many people have carried burdens of judgment and exclusion that they never deserved. Prejudices that take root in a culture can take a long time to untangle, and honesty requires us to admit that many of us, in one way or another, have shared in those biases. Recognizing that truth is one of the first steps toward a more just, compassionate, and truthful understanding of one another.

The writers of the New Testament were addressing specific behaviors within their own societies, many of which involved exploitation, violence, or abuse rather than the kinds of loving relationships people often discuss today. A fuller study of the original Greek can help us approach these passages with greater humility and historical awareness.

For example:

1. Arsenokoitai (ἀρσενοκοῖται)
   This rare Greek term appears in 1 Corinthians 6:9 and 1 Timothy 1:10. Scholars continue to debate its exact meaning. Many believe it referred to exploitative sexual behavior, such as men using others for sexual gain or participating in forms of prostitution, rather than describing loving same-sex relationships as we understand them today.

2. Malakoi (μαλακοί)
   Literally meaning "soft," this word was used in Greek culture to describe moral weakness, indulgence, or lack of self-discipline. In some historical contexts it referred to men who lived in luxury or who allowed themselves to be used sexually by others, often in exploitative arrangements.

3. Porneia (πορνεία)
   A broad Greek word usually translated as "sexual immorality." In the ancient world it covered a wide range of behaviors including prostitution, exploitation, and abuse. It did not function as a technical term describing sexual orientation.

4. Pathē atimias (πάθη ἀτιμίας)
   Found in Romans 1:26, this phrase is often translated "dishonorable passions." The language reflects behaviors considered excessive or degrading within the social practices

of the Roman world, many of which involved domination, power imbalance, or ritualized sexuality.

5. Eros (ἔρως) and Agapē (ἀγάπη)
    While the New Testament emphasizes agapē, meaning sacrificial love, Greek culture distinguished many forms of love. Understanding these distinctions reminds us that the Christian tradition ultimately measures relationships not merely by desire but by whether love reflects commitment, dignity, and care for the other person.

When Scripture is read within its historical language and cultural setting, it invites us not only to examine behavior but also to examine the motives of the heart. That was always Jesus' deeper concern.

ADDITIONAL RESOURCES

PFLAG (Parents, Families, and Friends of Lesbians and Gays)
PFLAG is a national organization dedicated to supporting, educating, and advocating for LGBTQ+ people and their families. With hundreds of local chapters, it provides community, guidance, and resources for those seeking greater understanding and compassionate support.
Website: **https://pflag.org**

APPENDIX

1. Robert Frost, poet, "The Pasture."
2. Abraham Maslow, "A Theory of Human Motivation," 1943. The principle that behavior is motivated is also reflected in the work of Freud and others.
3. Japanese Zen koans; various websites and Wikipedia entries.
4. Wikipedia, "Gay Leadership in the Catholic Church."
5. Wikipedia, "List of Christian denominations affirming LGBTQ people."
6. Hebrew Bible, Genesis 2:18.
7. Exegesis of certain Greek terms referring to immoral behaviors, understood by some scholars as not addressing sexual orientation per se. Workshop material from Hodges Boulevard Presbyterian Church, presented by the pastor at that time.
8. Julie Faith Parker, *SHAR*, June 2025, article on merisms.
9. Melissa Deckman, "Five Takeaways," PRRI Report, March 22, 2026.

www.ingramcontent.com/pod-product-compliance
Lightning Source LLC
Chambersburg PA
CBHW021125130726
47988CB00003B/1175